*To Chris –
for the magical summer of rings
and wheels and circles
J.H.*

*To my brother John
M.C.*

First published 1994
by Walker Books Ltd
87 Vauxhall Walk
London SE11 5HJ

2 4 6 8 10 9 7 5 3 1

Text © 1994 Judy Hindley
Illustrations © 1994 Margaret Chamberlain

This book has been typeset in Bembo.

Printed in Italy

British Library Cataloguing in Publication Data
A catalogue record for this book is
available from the British Library.
ISBN 0-7445-2553-5

WALKER BOOKS
LONDON

THE WHEELING AND WHIRLING-AROUND BOOK

Written by Judy Hindley

Illustrated by Margaret Chamberlain

Let us think for a bit about round things,

and things that spin and whirl –

things that wheel and reel and roll

and curve and coil and curl;

things that are round

like a ball is round,

and things that are round

like a wheel,

and things that swing

in orbital rings,

out and about

and back again;

When something
spins, two opposite things
are happening at once:
flying-apartness and
holding-togetherness.

Try this.
What would happen if you let go?

6

An orbit is the path of something travelling round something else.

7

and things you can

run your fingers round,

in a spiralling slope,

like an ice-cream cone;

and things you can hug,

like a tree.

Let us muse and gaze

and ponder,

and let our thoughts go free.

Let's give our eyes a wander,

and see what we can see!

Something dropped in the water makes it ripple into circles.

cone

cylinder

flat spiral

conical spiral

Every point on the rim of a circle is exactly the same distance from the centre.

Try this.
Draw a circle on paper and cut it out to make a paper disc. Now keep folding it in half...then open it out.

Do you see how all the folds meet in the centre?

A pizza is disc-shaped.

disc

WHERE'S MY HAT?

The imaginary line through a disc or sphere, round which it spins, is called its axis. Here's where the axis is on this disc.

A circular shape can do some things that other shapes can't do...

Let us begin

with things that spin

if you flip them along on the ground.

You can do it with coins and bottle tops,

you can do it with rings and crowns;

or dinner plates, or dustbin lids,

or the rim of your grandfather's hat…

You can race them or chase them or bowl them away

to be driven along by a breeze,

and they sometimes whizz quite a way, like that,

and go speeding along with ease,

till they finally falter and wibble and wobble and drop

on the side that's flat.

ghostly circle

ghostly arc

But what if you twirl

a thinnish disc

until it's a perfect blur?

You'll find what you've made

in a ghostly way

is the every-ways-round of a sphere –

ghostly sphere

ghostly ring

round like a pea

or a ping-pong ball,

or the eyes at the top of your face;

like marbles and cherries

and egg yolks and just about

everything orbiting way out in space!

13

Oh, a twirlable sphere is a great sort of shape,

but think what a terrible mess it can make!

Imagine a scatter of peas or pearls

or spherical sweets in a pack that's burst –

how perfectly ghastly to have in the street;

how disastrous to have on the stair!

For anything perfectly rollable

will be rolling to

everywhichwhere!

A sphere is the most common natural shape. Most huge things in the universe are spheres, like the billions of stars and planets in space.

Stars and planets are shaped into spheres by the holding-together force called gravity.

If you dumped all the water from a swimming-pool in space, it would become one vast water-drop. (Imagine diving in and out of it!)

Most of the tiniest natural things are spheres, like droplets and bubbles, and the eggs of zillions of small creatures.

Clinging and holding-togetherness makes droplets into spheres.

Rolling things about tends to make them round - like Plasticine rolled in the palms of your hands or pebbles rolled by the waves.

OH NO! YOU HAVE BROKEN MY NECKLACE!

15

So STOP

and consider again your disc,

the spinnable thing you started with.

What's the name of the similar thing

on the things you know that go?

On bikes and trikes and trucks and cars

and roller-skates and apple-carts –

A solid disc makes a very heavy wheel. Joining the rim to the hub with spokes makes a wheel much lighter – so you can speed it up and slow it down more easily.

and ANYthing that spins and turns
and trundles along on a track?
Well, of course!
What you've got,
when you give it a thought,
is a thing that is known as a
WHEEL.

An axle joins a pair of wheels.

A hub is at the centre of a wheel.

17

Now, unlike a ball or a globe or a sphere,

a wheel doesn't happen a lot by itself.

It has to be made by the hands or the tools

of a human, like me or like you.

And why do we bother to do such a thing?

Because of the way these remarkable shapes

will do what we want them to do.

You can yoke them on axles,

or link them on pulleys,

or fit them with spokes and dials and hubs

and pointers that spin from a circular nub,

and spools within, and sprocketed rims,

and tyres, fat or thin…

We could muse all day upon wheels and reels

and the magical tricks of cogs!

But now let us think how a disc or a wheel

is quite like a slice …

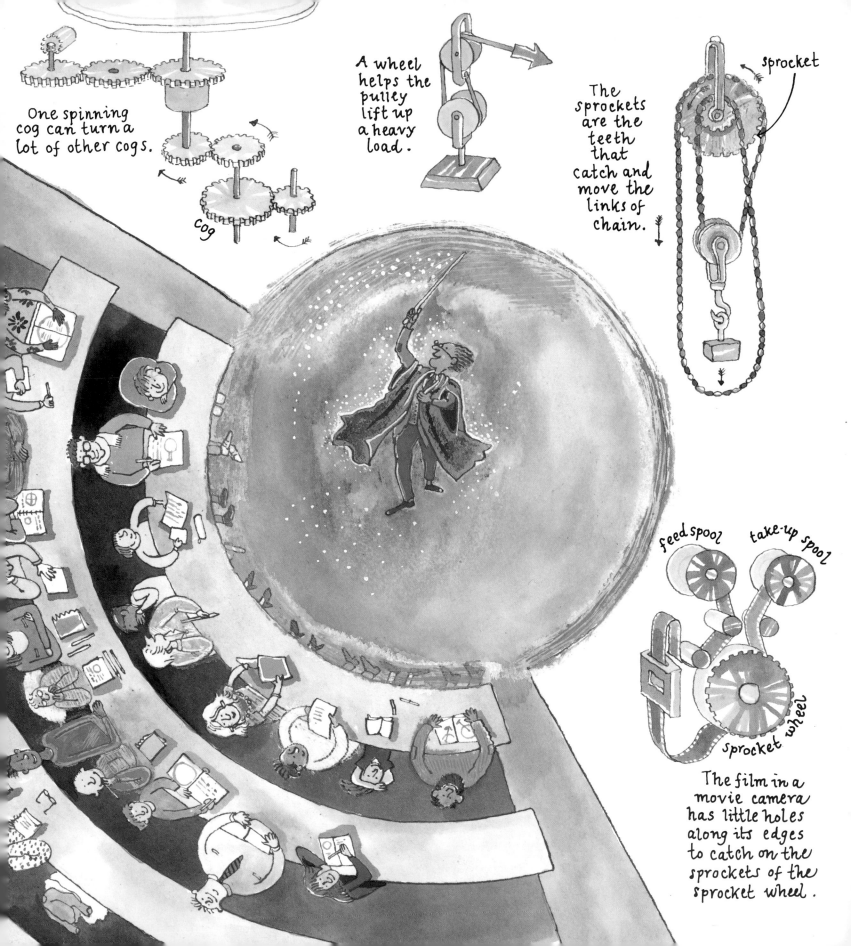

One spinning cog can turn a lot of other cogs.

cog

A wheel helps the pulley lift up a heavy load.

The sprockets are the teeth that catch and move the links of chain.

sprocket

feed spool take-up spool

sprocket wheel

The film in a movie camera has little holes along its edges to catch on the sprockets of the sprocket wheel.

of a log –

a long

cylindrical shape.

Now perfect cylinders,

smooth and straight,

are also usually human-made.

Just think about pencils

and candles,

and your grandmother's

rolling-pin;

and jars of a number of sizes

with a number of things within.

What about churns and urns, and tubs

in which the laundry spins?

Rollers are very useful cylindrical shapes... Logs were used to roll things before people thought of slicing them to make wheels.

Rollers are good for flattening roads.

A line of rollers can be used to make a conveyor belt.

A pair of rollers can squeeze and flatten wood pulp into paper.

20

What shape is a knitting needle?

And spools
and tubes and
drums and pipes
and drinking straws,
and the crown of a hat?
And what about pistons
and rollers and rods
that make an engine go?
Now…
you can see you can make
a cylindrical shape
out of wheel upon wheel upon wheel.
But what if you sliced the skin of it off
in a curling, coiling peel?

21

Instead of stacks of wheels and rings,

what you'd have is spiralling springs –

things that go round and up (or down)

like telephone cords or the springs in a bed.

Some are tight like the springs in a bike,

and some will stretch to the length of a line

and snap right back again!

But a spiralling curve can be also observed

in the coil of a snake or a butterfly's nose.

It can slope down the side

of a slide or a screw,

or circle us up in a stair –

A flat spiralling paper coil will drop into a loopy 3-D spiral if you hang it up. Try it and see!

can swoop us down, or whirl us up,

or carry us out and away –

can be flat as a spiral galaxy,

or the coil of a spider's web,

or go funnelling in

like a whirlwind

or water that glugs

from a tub.

No wonder

we yearn

to spin and turn

and go whirling

around

in rings –

from the tiniest atom

to weather and stars

there are so many

swirling

and orbiting

things...

Oh, let us dance

and sing!

It's not surprising we like to spin—like everything else, we're actually made of invisibly tiny spinning bits called atoms.

As well as spiral galaxies there are spherical, egg-shaped, and even blobby ones.

All the planets, moons and stars in the galaxy are spheres... The spinning Earth and its moon orbit the sun ... Our sun is a star in the arm of a spiralling galaxy like a great expanding Catherine wheel... Even the sun is spinning.

If you look through a powerful telescope, you can see the spiralling shapes of distant galaxies like ours.

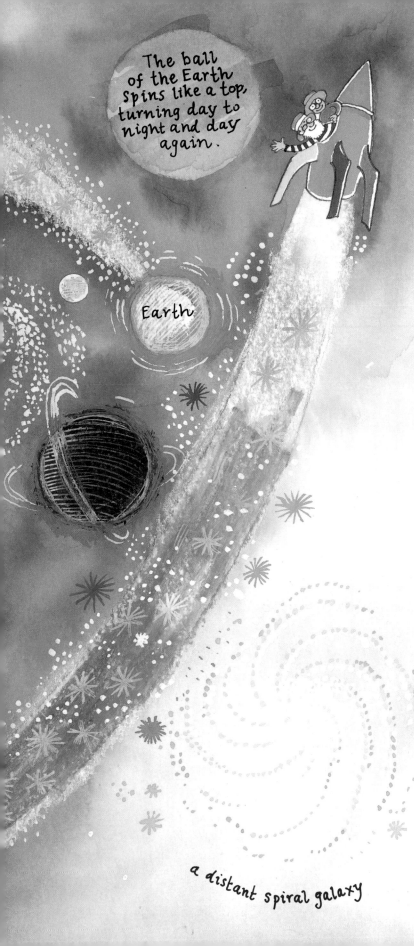

The ball of the Earth spins like a top, turning day to night and day again.

Earth

a distant spiral galaxy

Oh, here we go

round the day again,

and here we go round the sun,

and here we go round the galaxy

in the curl of its glittering arm!

See how the giddiest games

we play,

and the tiniest things there are,

echo out

through the travelling universe,

unravelling star by star –

and it's all a part

of the dance of things,

the spinning-aroundness

and spiralling rings,

however small, however near,

however vast and far…

29

Index

Look up the pages to find
out about all these wheeling and
whirling-around things. Don't forget
to look at both kinds of words:
this kind and this kind .